budgetbooks

BROADWAY SONGS

ISBN 0-634-04067-7

HAL•LEONARD®
CORPORATION

7777 W. BLUEMOUND RD. P.O. BOX 13819 MILWAUKEE, WI 53213

Visit Hal Leonard Online at
www.halleonard.com

CONTENTS

ALL GOOD GIFTS
from the Musical GODSPELL

Words and Music by
STEPHEN SCHWARTZ

thank you, Lord. _____ I want to thank you, Lord, _____

_____ thank _____ you, Lord.

ALONE AT THE DRIVE-IN MOVIE

from GREASE

Lyric and Music by WARREN CASEY
and JIM JACOBS

Might as well be in an ig - loo, _____

'Cause the heat - er does - n't work as good as

you. _____ (Ba - by come back.)

AND ALL THAT JAZZ

from CHICAGO

Words by FRED EBB
Music by JOHN KANDER

15

ANY DREAM WILL DO
from JOSEPH AND THE AMAZING TECHNICOLOR® DREAMCOAT

Music by ANDREW LLOYD WEBBER
Lyrics by TIM RICE

way ___ some - one was weep - ing, but the world was

sleep - ing, a - ny dream will do. I wore my

coat with gol - den lin - ing, bright col - ours

CHOIR

I wore my coat, ___ ah, ___

24

gin - ning, the light is dim - ming and the dream is

ah, _____ ah. _____

too, the world and I, we are still

The world and I, _____

wait - ing, still he - si - ta - ting a - ny dream will

ah, _____ ah. _____

ANYTHING YOU CAN DO
from the Stage Production ANNIE GET YOUR GUN

Words and Music by
IRVING BERLIN

I'm su-pe-ri-or, you're in-fe-ri-or.

I'm the big at-trac-tion, you're the small.___ I'm the ma-jor one,

you're the mi-nor one, I can beat you shoot-in', that's not all.___

Annie: An - y - thing you can do, I can do bet - ter.
Annie: An - y - thing you can buy, I can buy cheap - er.
Annie: An - y - thing you can lick, I can lick fast - er.

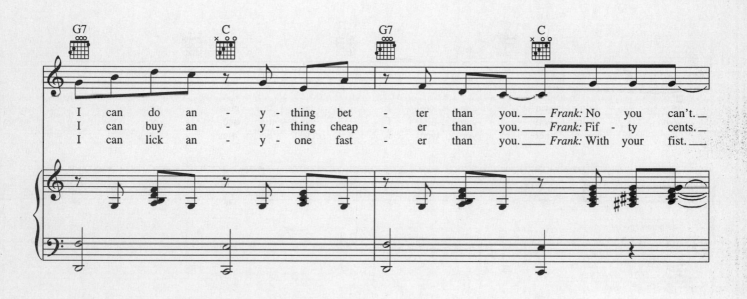

I can do an - y - thing bet - ter than you. ___ *Frank:* No you can't. ___
I can buy an - y - thing cheap - er than you. ___ *Frank:* Fif - ty cents. ___
I can lick an - y - one fast - er than you. ___ *Frank:* With your fist. ___

___ *Annie:* Yes I can. ___ *Frank:* No you can't. ___ *Annie:* Yes I can. ___ *Frank:* No you can't. ___
___ *Annie:* For - ty cents. ___ *Frank:* Thir - ty cents. ___ *Annie:* Twen - ty cents. ___ *Frank:* No you can't. ___
___ *Annie:* With my feet. ___ *Frank:* With your feet. ___ *Annie:* With an axe. ___ *Frank:* No you can't. ___

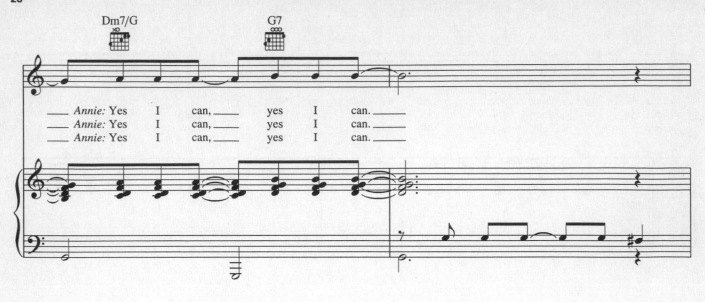

Annie: Yes I can,___ yes I can.___
Annie: Yes I can,___ yes I can.___
Annie: Yes I can,___ yes I can.___

An- y- thing you can be, I can be great- er.
An- y- thing you can dig, I can dig deep- er.
An- y school where you went I could be mas- ter.

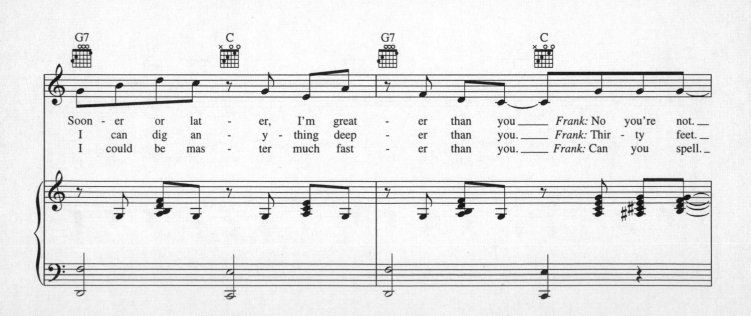

Soon- er or lat- er, I'm great- er than you ___ *Frank:* No you're not. ___
I can dig an- y- thing deep- er than you. ___ *Frank:* Thir- ty feet. ___
I could be mas- ter much fast- er than you. ___ *Frank:* Can you spell. ___

___ *Annie:* Yes I am. ___ *Frank:* No you're not. ___ *Annie:* Yes I am. ___ *Frank:* No you're not. ___
___ *Annie:* For - ty feet. ___ *Frank:* Fif - ty feet. ___ *Annie:* Six - ty feet. ___ *Frank:* No you can't. ___
___ *Annie:* No I can't. ___ *Frank:* Can you add. ___ *Annie:* No I can't. ___ *Frank:* Can you teach. ___

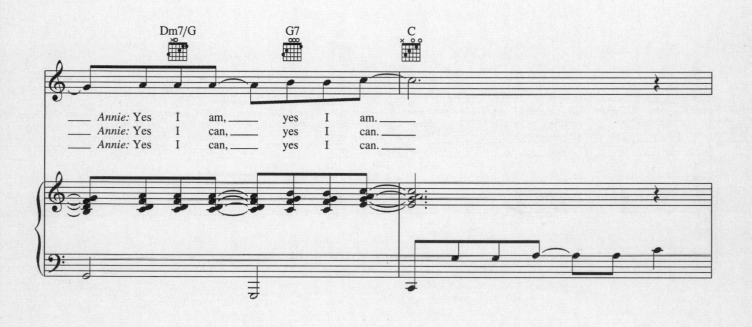

___ *Annie:* Yes I am, ___ yes I am. ___
___ *Annie:* Yes I can, ___ yes I can. ___
___ *Annie:* Yes I can, ___ yes I can. ___

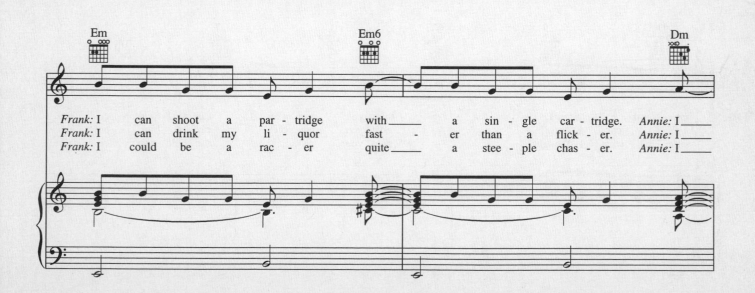

Frank: I can shoot a par - tridge with ___ a sin - gle car - tridge. *Annie:* I ___
Frank: I can drink my li - quor fast - er than a flick - er. *Annie:* I ___
Frank: I could be a rac - er quite ___ a stee - ple chas - er. *Annie:* I ___

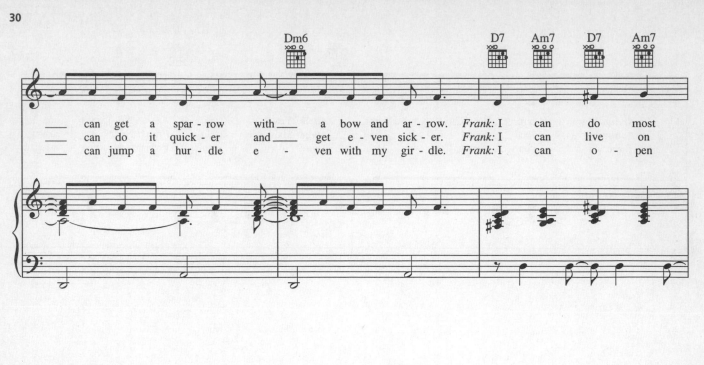

___ can get a spar - row with___ a bow and ar - row. *Frank:* I can do most
___ can do it quick - er and___ get e - ven sick - er. *Frank:* I can live on
___ can jump a hur - dle e - ven with my gir - dle. *Frank:* I can o - pen

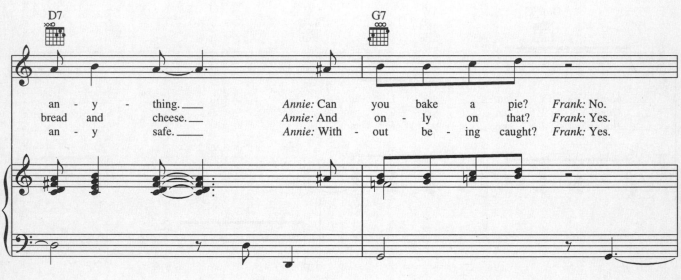

an - y - thing.___ *Annie:* Can you bake a pie? *Frank:* No.
bread and cheese.___ *Annie:* And on - ly on that? *Frank:* Yes.
an - y safe.___ *Annie:* With - out be - ing caught? *Frank:* Yes.

Annie: Neith - er can I. An - y - thing you can sing I can sing loud - er.
Annie: So can a rat. An - y note you can reach, I can go high - er.
Annie: That's what I thought. An - y note you can hold I can hold long - er.

AS LONG AS HE NEEDS ME

from the Columbia Pictures - Romulus Motion Picture Production of Lionel Bart's OLIVER!

Words and Music by
LIONEL BART

BAUBLES, BANGLES AND BEADS

from KISMET

Words and Music by ROBERT WRIGHT
and GEORGE FORREST
(Music Based on Themes of A. BORODIN)

BEING ALIVE

from COMPANY

Music and Lyrics by
STEPHEN SONDHEIM

Add notes in parentheses 2nd time only.

38

live.

ff

(♩=112)

p

Some-bod - y hold me too   close,
Some-bod - y need me too   much,

Some-bod - y hurt me too
Some-bod - y know me too

*

deep,
well;

Some-bod - y sit in my   chair   And ru - in my
Some-bod - y pull me up   short   And put me through

* Add notes in parentheses 2nd time only.

43

44

THE BEST OF TIMES
from LA CAGE AUX FOLLES

Music and Lyric by
JERRY HERMAN

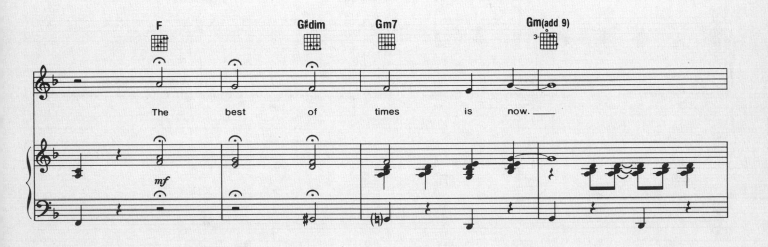

The best of times is now. ____

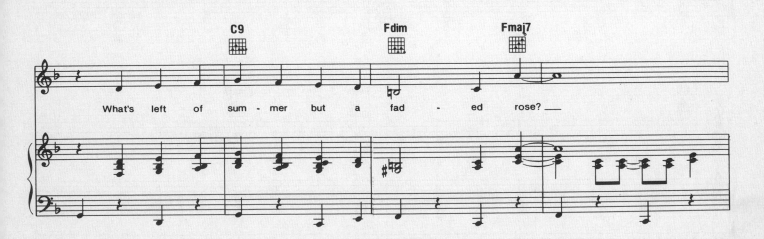

What's left of sum-mer but a fad-ed rose? ____

48

BROADWAY BABY
from FOLLIES

Words and Music by
STEPHEN SONDHEIM

57

58

CABARET
from the Musical CABARET

Words by FRED EBB
Music by JOHN KANDER

A COCKEYED OPTIMIST
from SOUTH PACIFIC

Lyrics by OSCAR HAMMERSTEIN II
Music by RICHARD RODGERS

When the sky is a bright can-ar-y yel-low I for-get ev-'ry cloud I've ev-er seen, So they call me a cock-eyed op-ti-mist Im-ma-ture and in-

CONSIDER YOURSELF

from the Columbia Pictures - Romulus Motion Picture Production of Lionel Bart's OLIVER!

Words and Music by
LIONEL BART

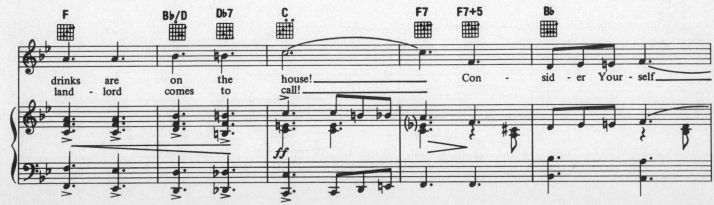

73

74

EVERYTHING'S COMING UP ROSES
from GYPSY

Words by STEPHEN SONDHEIM
Music by JULE STYNE

FALLING IN LOVE WITH LOVE
from THE BOYS FROM SYRACUSE

Words by LORENZ HART
Music by RICHARD RODGERS

85

FOOTLOOSE

from the Broadway Musical FOOTLOOSE

Words by DEAN PITCHFORD and KENNY LOGGINS
Music by KENNY LOGGINS

This edition may be sung by a solo singer. The song appears in a different form in the show, accommodating various singers' entrances.

89

that time's just hold - ing me down. _____ (I hate this

feel - ing; time is hold - ing me down. _____)

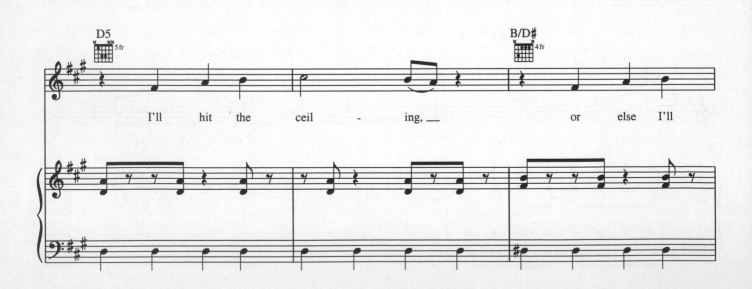

I'll hit the ceil - ing, ___ or else I'll

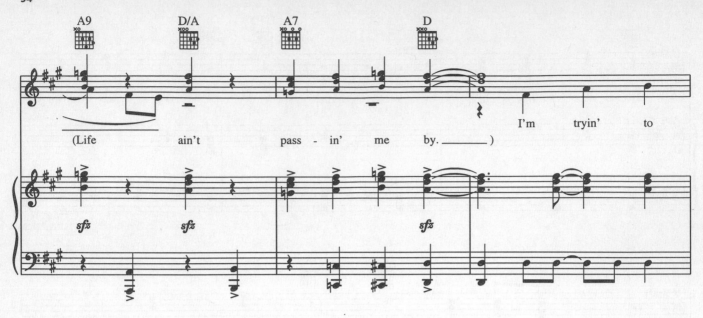

(Life ain't pass-in' me by. _____) I'm tryin' to

tell you _____ it will if you don't e-ven

try. (You can fly, _____ you can fly, _____ you can fly, _____

GETTING TO KNOW YOU

from THE KING AND I

Lyrics by OSCAR HAMMERSTEIN II
Music by RICHARD RODGERS

GUS: THE THEATRE CAT
from CATS

Music by ANDREW LLOYD WEBBER
Text by T.S. ELIOT

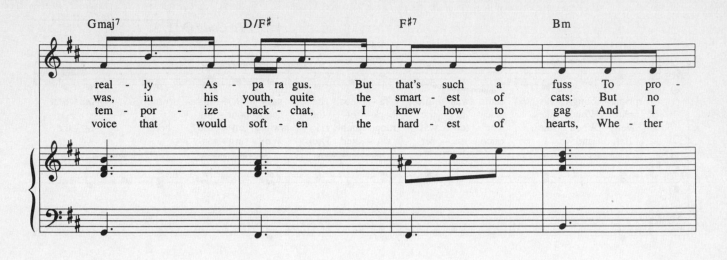

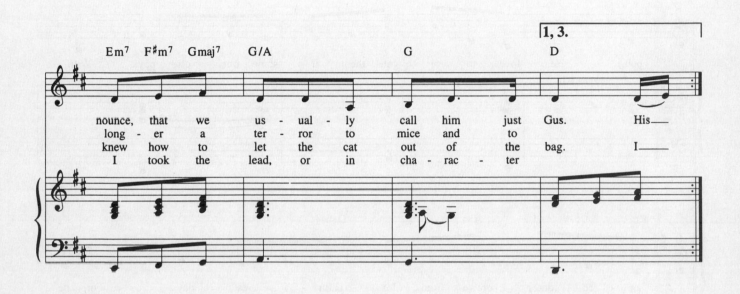

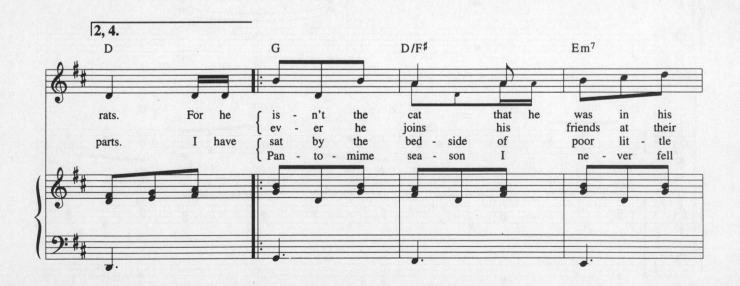

104

GUS (Sung reprise)
And I once crossed the stage on a telegraph wire,
To rescue a child when a house was on fire.
And I think that I still can much better than most,
Produced blood-curdling noises to bring on the Ghost.
I once played Growltiger, could do it again...

THE HOSTESS WITH THE MOSTES' ON THE BALL

from the Stage Production CALL ME MADAM

Words and Music by
IRVING BERLIN

SALLY:

I was born on a thou-sand a-cres of Ok-la-ho-ma land.

Noth-ing grew on the thou-sand a-cres for it was grav-el and sand.

One day Fa-ther start-ed dig-ging in a field Hop-ing to find some

slight rit.

soil. He dug and he dug and what do you think? Oil, oil,

slight rit.

oil. The mon-ey rolled in and I rolled out with a for-tune piled so high._

Wash - ing - ton was my des - ti - na - tion And now who am

Medium Bounce tempo

I?_____ I'm the cho - sen par - ty giv - er for the

White House cli - en - tele ___ And they know that I de - liv - er What it

takes to make 'em jell. ___ And in Wash - ing - ton I'm known _ by one and all _

___ As the host - ess with the mos - tes' on the ball. _

___ They would go to El - sa Max - well, When they

112

best that can be found ___ And a large a - mount ___ in my bank ac - count ___ When e -

lec - tion time comes 'round. ___ If you're feel - ing pres - i - den - tial You can

make it, yes, in - deed, ___ There are just three things es - sen - tial Let me

tell you all you need ___ Is an ounce of wis - dom and ___ a pound of gall ___

best time of his life, ___ E - ven bring his new af - fair ___ down, In - tro-

duce her as his wife. ___ But she must - n't leave her pan - ties in the

hall _____ For the host - ess who's the host - ess, with the mos - tes'

on the ball. _____

GUYS AND DOLLS
from GUYS AND DOLLS

By FRANK LOESSER

HONEY BUN

from SOUTH PACIFIC

Lyrics by OSCAR HAMMERSTEIN II
Music by RICHARD RODGERS

I AIN'T DOWN YET
from THE UNSINKABLE MOLLY BROWN

By MEREDITH WILLSON

123

I DREAMED A DREAM

from LES MISÉRABLES

Music by CLAUDE-MICHEL SCHÖNBERG
Lyrics by HERBERT KRETZMER
Original Text by ALAIN BOUBLIL and JEAN-MARC NATEL

I ENJOY BEING A GIRL
from FLOWER DRUM SONG

Lyrics by OSCAR HAMMERSTEIN II
Music by RICHARD RODGERS

LET IT GO

from THE FULL MONTY

Words and Music by
DAVID YAZBEK

137

I HAVE DREAMED
from THE KING AND I

Lyrics by OSCAR HAMMERSTEIN II
Music by RICHARD RODGERS

I WILL NEVER LEAVE YOU

from SIDE SHOW

Words by BILL RUSSELL
Music by HENRY KRIEGER

I'M A WOMAN

from SMOKEY JOE'S CAFE

Words and Music by JERRY LEIBER
and MIKE STOLLER

Spoken:
I can wash out forty-four pairs of socks and have them hangin' out on the line,
I can rub and scrub till this old house is shinin' like a dime,
If you come to me sickly, you know I'm gonna make you well,
I can stretch a greenback dollar bill from here to kingdom come.

I can starch and iron two dozen shirts before you can count from one to nine,
Feed the baby, grease the car and powder my face at the same time,
If you come to me hexed up, you know I'm gonna break the spell,
I can play the numbers, pay my bills, and still end up with some.

I can scoop up a great big dipper full of lard from the drippin's can,
Get all dressed up, go out and swing till four a.m. and then
If you come to me hungry, I'm gonna fill you full o' grits,
I got a twenty dollar gold piece says there ain't nothing I can't do.

Throw it in the skillet, go out and do my shopping and be back before it melts in the pan,
Lay down at five, jump up at six and start all over again,
If it's love you're lackin', I'll kiss you and give you the shiverin' fits,
I can make a dress out of a feedbag and I can make a man out of you,

Sung: 'Cause I'm a

wom - an, __ dou-ble u-o - m-a-n. __ I'll say it a-

gain. gain. 'Cause I'm a wom - an, __

dou-ble u-o - m-a-n. __

I'VE GROWN ACCUSTOMED TO HER FACE

from MY FAIR LADY

Words by ALAN JAY LERNER
Music by FREDERICK LOEWE

IF HE WALKED INTO MY LIFE

from MAME

Music and Lyric by
JERRY HERMAN

IF I CAN'T LOVE HER

from Walt Disney's BEAUTY AND THE BEAST: THE BROADWAY MUSICAL

Music by ALAN MENKEN
Lyrics by TIM RICE

162

163

THE IMPOSSIBLE DREAM
(The Quest)
from MAN OF LA MANCHA

Lyric by JOE DARION
Music by MITCH LEIGH

170

171

KANSAS CITY
from OKLAHOMA!

Lyrics by OSCAR HAMMERSTEIN II
Music by RICHARD RODGERS

174

176

LEANING ON A LAMP POST

from ME AND MY GIRL

By NOEL GAY

LET'S HAVE ANOTHER CUP O' COFFEE

from the Stage Production FACE THE MUSIC

Words and Music by
IRVING BERLIN

183

LOVE CHANGES EVERYTHING

from ASPECTS OF LOVE

Music by ANDREW LLOYD WEBBER
Lyrics by DON BLACK and CHARLES HART

Off ___ in- to the world we go, plan-ning fu-tures, shap-ing years.

Love ___ bursts in and sud-den-ly, all our wis-dom dis-ap-pears.

Love ___ makes fools of ev- ery-one: all the rules we make are

LOVE, LOOK AWAY

from FLOWER DRUM SONG

Lyrics by OSCAR HAMMERSTEIN II
Music by RICHARD RODGERS

MAMA SAYS

from the Broadway Musical FOOTLOOSE

Words by DEAN PITCHFORD
Music by TOM SNOW

MAMA, A RAINBOW

from MINNIE'S BOYS

Lyrics by HAL HACKADY
Music by LARRY GROSSMAN

202

MAME
from MAME

Music and Lyric by
JERRY HERMAN

With a lilt

Chorus

1. You coax the blues right out__ of the horn, Mame,____
2. You've brought the cake-walk back__ in-to style, Mame,____

You charm the husk right off__ of the corn, Mame,____
You make the weep-in' wil-low tree smile, Mame,____

You've got the ban-joes strum-min' and plunk-in' out a tune to beat the
Your skin is Dix-ie sat-in, there's reb-el in your man-ner and your

MEMORY
from CATS

Music by ANDREW LLOYD WEBBER
Text by TREVOR NUNN after T.S. ELIOT

208

209

210

MAYBE THIS TIME
from the Musical CABARET

Words by FRED EBB
Music by JOHN KANDER

214

MY CUP RUNNETH OVER

from I DO! I DO!

Words by TOM JONES
Music by HARVEY SCHMIDT

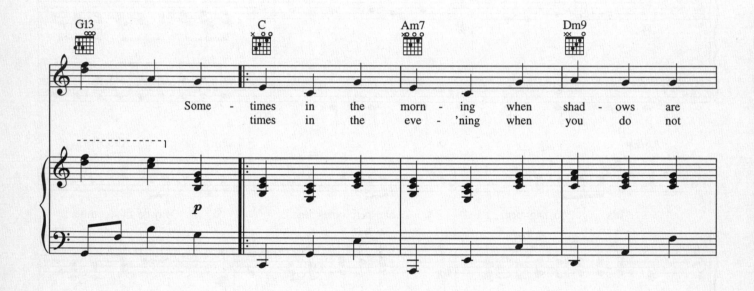

Some- times in the morn- ing when shad- ows are

times in the eve - 'ning when you do not

deep, I lie here be - side you, just watch- ing you

see, I stud - y the small things you do con - stant -

NO OTHER LOVE

from ME AND JULIET

Lyrics by OSCAR HAMMERSTEIN II
Music by RICHARD RODGERS

How far a-way are you? How man-y lone-ly sighs, dear? How man-y weep-ing skies, dear? How far a-way are you? How long have I to go?

OKLAHOMA

from OKLAHOMA!

Lyrics by OSCAR HAMMERSTEIN II
Music by RICHARD RODGERS

ON BROADWAY
from SMOKEY JOE'S CAFE

Words and Music by BARRY MANN, CYNTHIA WEIL,
MIKE STOLLER and JERRY LEIBER

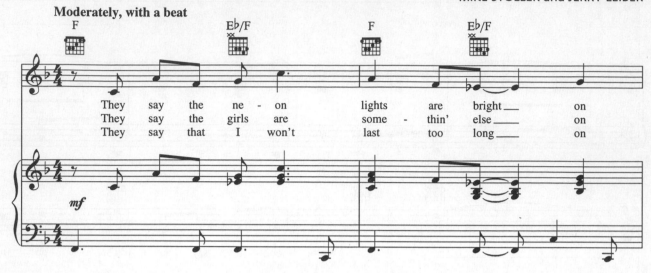

They say the ne - on lights are bright___ on
They say the girls are some - thin' else___ on
They say that I won't last too long___ on

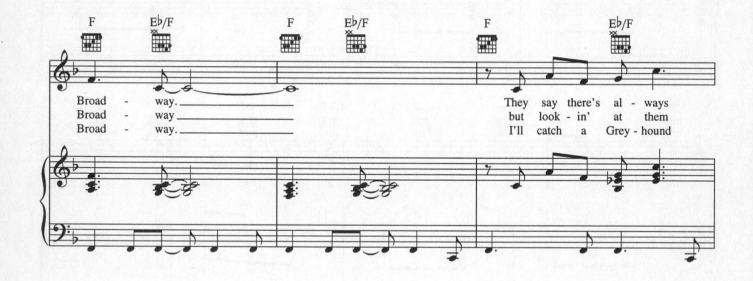

Broad - way. _____ They say there's al - ways
Broad - way. _____ but look - in' at them
Broad - way. _____ I'll catch a Grey - hound

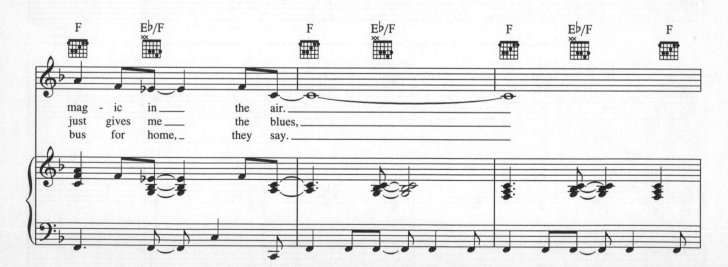

mag - ic in ___ the air. _____
just gives me ___ the blues, _____
bus for home, _ they say. _____

ONE
from A CHORUS LINE

Music by MARVIN HAMLISCH
Lyric by EDWARD KLEBAN

THE RAIN IN SPAIN
from MY FAIR LADY

Words by ALAN JAY LERNER
Music by FREDERICK LOEWE

People

from FUNNY GIRL

Words by BOB MERRILL
Music by JULE STYNE

PROLOGUE: THE OLD RED HILLS OF HOME

from PARADE

Music and Lyrics by
JASON ROBERT BROWN

244

RIVER IN THE RAIN

from BIG RIVER

Words and Music by
ROGER MILLER

SO IN LOVE

from KISS ME, KATE

Words and Music by
COLE PORTER

Strange, dear, _____ but true, dear, _____ When I'm close _____ to you, dear, _____

love   with   you,   my   love _____   am

THE SOUND OF MUSIC

from THE SOUND OF MUSIC

Lyrics by OSCAR HAMMERSTEIN II
Music by RICHARD RODGERS

Molto moderato *(tenderly)*

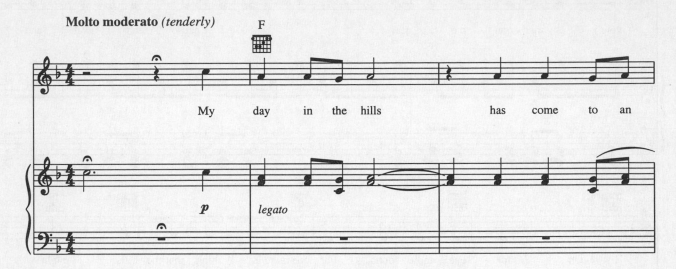

My day in the hills has come to an

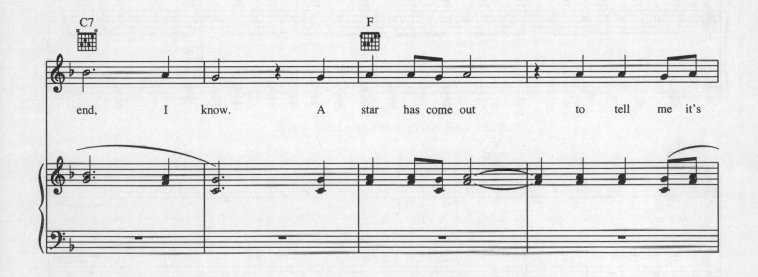

end, I know. A star has come out to tell me it's

time to go. But deep in the dark green shad-ows are

STAYIN' ALIVE
from the Broadway Musical SATURDAY NIGHT FEVER

Words and Music by BARRY GIBB,
MAURICE GIBB and ROBIN GIBB

SUN AND MOON
from MISS SAIGON

Music by CLAUDE-MICHEL SCHÖNBERG
Lyrics by RICHARD MALTBY JR. and ALAIN BOUBLIL
Adapted from original French Lyrics by ALAIN BOUBLIL

SUMMER NIGHTS

from GREASE

Lyric and Music by WARREN CASEY
and JIM JACOBS

SUPPER TIME
from the Stage Production AS THOUSANDS CHEER

Words and Music by
IRVING BERLIN

Supper time, ___ I should set the ta - ble 'cause it's sup - per time. ___

Some-how I'm not a - ble 'cause that man o' - mine ___ ain't com-in' home ___ no

THE SURREY WITH THE FRINGE ON TOP

from OKLAHOMA!

Lyrics by OSCAR HAMMERSTEIN II
Music by RICHARD RODGERS

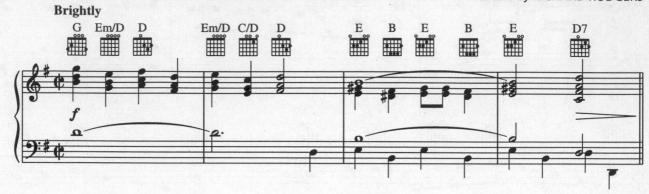

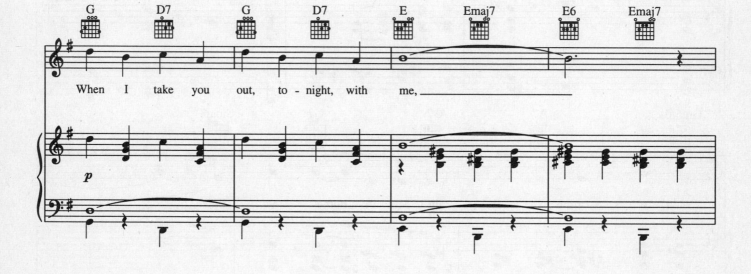

When I take you out, to-night, with me, _____

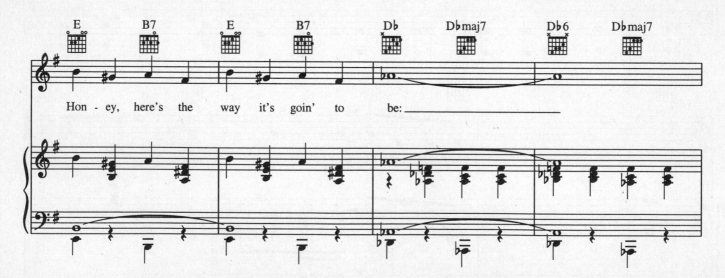

Hon - ey, here's the way it's goin' to be: _____

284

286

THE SWEETEST SOUNDS
from NO STRINGS

Lyrics and Music by
RICHARD RODGERS

THE TALE OF THE OYSTER

from FIFTY MILLION FRENCHMEN

Words and Music by
COLE PORTER

TEN CENTS A DANCE
from SIMPLE SIMON

Words by LORENZ HART
Music by RICHARD RODGERS

8vb

299

THERE'S A SMALL HOTEL
from ON YOUR TOES

Words by LORENZ HART
Music by RICHARD RODGERS

Moderately

There's a small ho-tel With a wish-ing well; I wish that we were there to-geth-er. _____ There's a brid-al suite; One room bright and neat, Com-

302

THERE'S NO BUSINESS LIKE SHOW BUSINESS

from the Stage Production ANNIE GET YOUR GUN

Words and Music by
IRVING BERLIN

THIS IS THE MOMENT
from JEKYLL & HYDE

Words by LESLIE BRICUSSE
Music by FRANK WILDHORN

Slowly

This is the

mo-ment,_____ this is the day, when I send all my doubts and de-mons____ on their

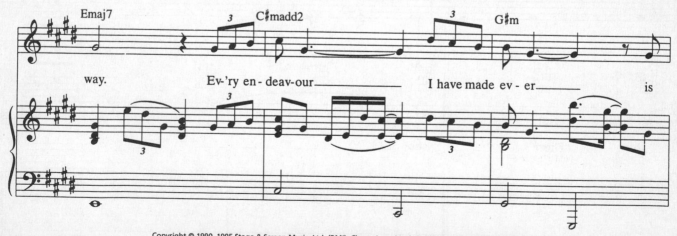

way. Ev-'ry en-deav-our_____ I have made ev-er_____ is

314

TILL THERE WAS YOU

from Meredith Willson's THE MUSIC MAN

By MEREDITH WILLSON

TURN BACK, O MAN
from the Musical GODSPELL

Words and Music by
STEPHEN SCHWARTZ

(Can ya take it?) For-swear thy__ fool-ish__ ways.__ (See ya later—
(Hiya big boy)

I'm going to the front of the the-a-ter.)

Soft, Folk feeling

(Jesus:) Earth shall be fair, and

molto legato

all her peo-ple one. Nor till that hour shall God's whole

A WONDERFUL DAY LIKE TODAY

from THE ROAR OF THE GREASEPAINT—
THE SMELL OF THE CROWD

Words and Music by LESLIE BRICUSSE
and ANTHONY NEWLEY

The sec-ond I saw it I knew, I said to my-self, "A-ha" I could tell at a glance That it was-n't by chance That we hap-pen to be where we are. From the

WAITIN' FOR THE LIGHT TO SHINE

from BIG RIVER

Words and Music by
ROGER MILLER

329

WHO WILL LOVE ME AS I AM?

from SIDE SHOW

Words by BILL RUSSELL
Music by HENRY KRIEGER

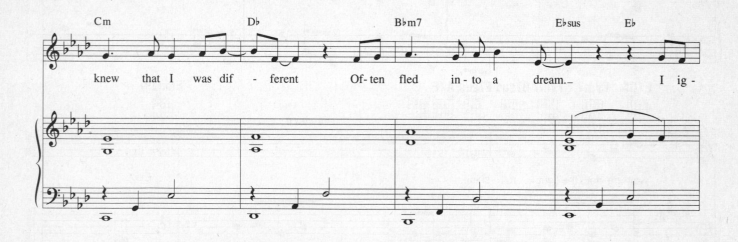

WISH YOU WERE HERE

from WISH YOU WERE HERE

Words and Music by
HAROLD ROME

Tempo di Beguine

Where ___ is the won - der as each ___ day would start That sang ___ with the dawn, ___ ran a- way ___ with my heart? Where is it gone? ___

339

WITH A SONG IN MY HEART

from SPRING IS HERE

Words by LORENZ HART
Music by RICHARD RODGERS

WITH ONE LOOK

from SUNSET BOULEVARD

Music by ANDREW LLOYD WEBBER
Lyrics by DON BLACK and CHRISTOPHER HAMPTON,
with contributions by AMY POWERS

NORMA With one look I can break your heart, with one look I play ev - ery part.

I can make your sad heart sing. With one look you'll know all you need to know.

With one smile I'm the girl next door or the love that you've hun - gered for.

YOU'LL NEVER WALK ALONE

from CAROUSEL

Lyrics by OSCAR HAMMERSTEIN II
Music by RICHARD RODGERS

* alternate lyric: hold your head up high

Get more BANG for your buck!
with budgetbooks

These value-priced collections feature **352 pages** of **piano/vocal/guitar** arrangements. With over **70 hit songs** in each book for only **$12.95**, you pay **18 cents or less for each song!**

BROADWAY SONGS

This jam-packed collection features 73 songs from 56 shows, including *Annie Get Your Gun, Beauty and the Beast, Cabaret, The Full Monty, Jekyll & Hyde, Les Misérables, The Music Man, Oklahoma!,* and more. Songs include: Any Dream Will Do • Cabaret • Consider Yourself • Footloose • Getting to Know You • I Dreamed a Dream • The Impossible Dream (The Quest) • Love Changes Everything • One • People • Summer Nights • The Surrey with the Fringe on Top • With One Look • You'll Never Walk Alone • and more.
00310832 P/V/G $12.95

COUNTRY SONGS

A great collection of 90 songs, including: Abilene • All My Ex's Live in Texas • Always on My Mind • Amazed • Blue Eyes Crying in the Rain • Boot Scootin' Boogie • Breathe • By the Time I Get to Phoenix • The Chair • Cowboy Take Me Away • Down at the Twist and Shout • Elvira • Friends in Low Places • The Greatest Man I Never Knew • Help Me Make It Through the Night • Hey, Good Lookin' • Lucille • Mammas Don't Let Your Babies Grow Up to Be Cowboys • Okie from Muskogee • Sixteen Tons • Walkin' After Midnight • You Are My Sunshine • and many more!
00310833 P/V/G $12.95

JAZZ STANDARDS

A collection of over 80 jazz classics. Includes: Alfie • Alright, Okay, You Win • Always in My Heart (Siempre En Mi Corazón) • Autumn in New York • Bewitched • Blue Skies • Body and Soul • Cherokee (Indian Love Song) • Do Nothin' Till You Hear from Me • Fever • Fly Me to the Moon (In Other Words) • Good Morning Heartache • Harlem Nocturne • I'll Be Seeing You • In the Mood • Isn't It Romantic? • Lazy Afternoon • Lover • Manhattan • Mona Lisa • Stella by Starlight • When Sunny Gets Blue • and more.
00310830 P/V/G $12.95

LOVE SONGS

This collection of over 70 favorite love songs includes: And I Love Her • Crazy • Endless Love • Fields of Gold • I Just Called to Say I Love You • I'll Be There • Longer • (You Make Me Feel Like) A Natural Woman • Still • Wonderful Tonight • You Are So Beautiful • You Are the Sunshine of My Life • and more.
00310834 P/V/G $12.95

MOVIE SONGS

Over 70 memorable movie moments, including: Almost Paradise • Also Sprach Zarathustra, Opening Theme • Cole's Song • The Crying Game • Funny Girl • I Say a Little Prayer • Il Postino (The Postman) • Jailhouse Rock • Psycho (Prelude) • Puttin' On the Ritz • She • Southampton • Take My Breath Away (Love Theme) • Theme from "Terms of Endearment" • Up Where We Belong • The Way We Were • Where the Boys Are • and more.
00310831 P/V/G $12.95

POP/ROCK

This great collection of 75 top pop hits features: Adia • Angel • Back in the High Life Again • Barbara Ann • Crimson and Clover • Don't Cry Out Loud • Dust in the Wind • Hero • I Hope You Dance • If You're Gone • Jack and Diane • Lady Marmalade • Mony, Mony • Respect • Stand by Me • Tequila • Vision of Love • We Got the Beat • What's Going On • You Sang to Me • and more!
00310835 P/V/G $12.95

FOR MORE INFORMATION, SEE YOUR LOCAL MUSIC DEALER, OR WRITE TO:

HAL•LEONARD®
CORPORATION

7777 W. BLUEMOUND RD. P.O. BOX 13819 MILWAUKEE, WI 53213

Visit Hal Leonard Online at
www.halleonard.com

Prices, contents & availability subject to change without notice.

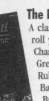

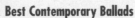